M000189832

YAS QUEEN

summersdale

YAS QUEEN

An Hachette UK Company
www.hachette.co.uk

Summersdale Publishers Ltd
Part of Octopus Publishing Group Limited
Carmelite House
50 Victoria Embankment
LONDON
EC4Y 0DZ
UK

www.summersdale.com

Printed and bound in China

ISBN: 978-1-78783-534-4

Substantial discounts on bulk quantities of Summersdale books are available to corporations, professional associations and other organizations. For details contact general enquiries: telephone: +44 (0) 1243 771107 or email: enquiries@summersdale.com.

TO ....

FROM ....

THINK LIKE A QUEEN.
A QUEEN IS NOT
AFRAID TO FAIL.
FAILURE IS ANOTHER
STEPPING STONE
TO GREATNESS.

OPRAH WINFREY

LIFE IS A GREAT BIG CANVAS; THROW ALL THE PAINT ON IT YOU CAN.

DANNY KAYE

Bad vibes
don't go with
my outfit

Be loud about the things that are important to you.

KAREN WALROND

WHEN LIFE PUTS
YOU IN TOUGH
SITUATIONS, DON'T
SAY "WHY ME?",
SAY "TRY ME".

MILEY CYRUS

FIND OUT WHO
YOU ARE AND DO
IT ON PURPOSE.

DOLLY PARTON

GO
forth
AND BE
fierce

WE ARE ALL
OF US STARS,
AND WE DESERVE
TO TWINKLE.

MARILYN MONROE

KEEP
YOUR HEELS,
HEAD AND
STANDARDS
HIGH.

COCO CHANEL

LESS BITTER, MORE GLITTER

YOU BEING YOUR
TRUE SELF ISN'T GOING
TO OFFEND ANYBODY...
IF THEY'RE CONCERNED,
THAT'S ON THEM.

TAN FRANCE

DON'T YOU EVER LET A
SOUL IN THE WORLD TELL
YOU THAT YOU CAN'T BE
EXACTLY WHO YOU ARE.

LADY GAGA

I prefer to shock rather than to bore through repetition.

YVES SAINT LAURENT

A SASS A DAY KEEPS THE BASICS AWAY

THE MISFITS, THE
FREAKS, THE ONES
WHO FEEL LIKE
THEY DON'T HAVE
A PLACE... YOU GOT
IT. JUST BE YOU.

MICHELLE VISAGE

WHATEVER
YOU'RE THINKING,
THINK BIGGER.

TONY HSIEH

WORK IT, QUEEN!

NOTHING I ACCEPT
ABOUT MYSELF CAN
BE USED AGAINST ME
TO DIMINISH ME.

AUDRE LORDE

BE YOURSELF.
EVERYONE
ELSE IS TAKEN.

ANONYMOUS

YOU SHOULD ALWAYS
SPEAK YOUR MIND,
AND BE BOLD, AND
BE OBNOXIOUS,
AND DO WHATEVER
YOU WANT.

CHELSEA HANDLER

YOU ARE MADE OF STARDUST, WISHES AND MAGICAL THINGS

STORM?
SHINE YOUR
LIGHT AND MAKE
A RAINBOW.

RICHIE NORTON

BEAUTY IS NOT JUST PHYSICAL. IT'S ABOUT WHAT YOU STAND FOR, HOW YOU LIVE YOUR LIFE.

HALLE BERRY

Queens
don't
compete

I will not be ignored. I am here to stay.

RuPAUL

IF SOMETHING
DOESN'T
LOOK RIGHT,
THROW SOME
GLITTER ON IT.

ADAM LAMBERT

AM I
GOOD ENOUGH?
YES I AM.

MICHELLE OBAMA

THIS
GIRL
CAN

CONFIDENCE IS
THE SEXIEST
THING TO HAVE.

JESSIE J

EAT
DIAMONDS
FOR BREAKFAST
AND SHINE
ALL DAY.

ANONYMOUS

TOO GLAM
TO GIVE
A DAMN

**DON'T BE PUSHED
AROUND BY THE FEARS
IN YOUR MIND.
BE LED BY THE DREAMS
IN YOUR HEART.**

ROY T. BENNETT

ACCEPT NO ONE'S DEFINITION OF YOUR LIFE; DEFINE YOURSELF.

HARVEY FIERSTEIN

Different is good.
So don't fit in.
Don't sit still.
Don't ever try
to be less than
what you are.

ANGELINA JOLIE

THROW SASS AROUND LIKE CONFETTI

ALWAYS BE A
FIRST-RATE VERSION
OF YOURSELF,
INSTEAD OF A
SECOND-RATE
VERSION OF
SOMEBODY ELSE.

JUDY GARLAND

IT TAKES A
LONG TIME TO GET
TO BE A DIVA...
YOU GOTTA
WORK AT IT.

DIANA ROSS

STAY

focused

AND

sparkly

BETTER A DIAMOND
WITH A FLAW THAN
A PEBBLE WITHOUT.

CHINESE PROVERB

BEWARE;
FOR I AM
FEARLESS, AND
THEREFORE
POWERFUL.

MARY SHELLEY

EMBRACE YOUR WEIRDNESS.

CARA DELEVINGNE

WERK IT, SIS

THERE'S NO BETTER MAKE-UP THAN SELF-CONFIDENCE.

SHAKIRA

You are
your own
queen.

NIKITA GILL

BE SAVAGE, NOT AVERAGE

BETTER TO
LIVE ONE YEAR
AS A TIGER,
**THAN A HUNDRED
AS A SHEEP.**

MADONNA

YOU CANNOT
MAKE A DIFFERENCE
UNLESS YOU'RE
DIFFERENT.

JUSTIN TIMBERLAKE

EITHER YOU RUN THE DAY OR THE DAY RUNS YOU.

JIM ROHN

Be a
goal-getter

NEVER DULL
YOUR SHINE FOR
SOMEBODY ELSE.

TYRA BANKS

I'VE BEEN
THROUGH IT
ALL, BABY.
I'M MOTHER
COURAGE.

ELIZABETH TAYLOR

DARLING,
YOU ARE
FABULOUS

THOUGH SHE BE BUT LITTLE, SHE IS FIERCE.

WILLIAM SHAKESPEARE

If they don't like you for being yourself, be yourself even more.

TAYLOR SWIFT

MAKE THEM NEVER BE ABLE TO IMAGINE WHAT LIFE WITHOUT YOU THERE WOULD BE LIKE.

ROSS MATHEWS

CONFIDENCE LEVEL: STRATOSPHERIC

YOU'RE NOT
GONNA TELL ME
WHO I AM.
I'M GONNA TELL
YOU WHO I AM.

NICKI MINAJ

DO YOUR
THING AND
DON'T CARE IF
THEY LIKE IT.

TINA FEY

TGIF: THANK GOD I'M FABULOUS

YOU'RE STRONG.
YOU'RE A KELLY
CLARKSON SONG.
YOU'VE GOT THIS.

JONATHAN VAN NESS

DARE TO BE
DIFFERENT AND
TO SET YOUR OWN
PATTERN, LIVE YOUR
OWN LIFE AND
FOLLOW YOUR
OWN STAR.

WILFERD PETERSON

NOTE TO SELF: NEVER LEAVE HOME WITHOUT GLITTER.

ADRIENNE KRESS

Always
have class,
but always
kick ass

Not today, Satan.

BIANCA DEL RIO

LOVE YOUR FLAWS.
OWN YOUR QUIRKS.
AND KNOW THAT YOU
ARE JUST AS PERFECT
AS ANYONE ELSE,
EXACTLY AS YOU ARE.

ARIANA GRANDE

BE
the
GAME
changer

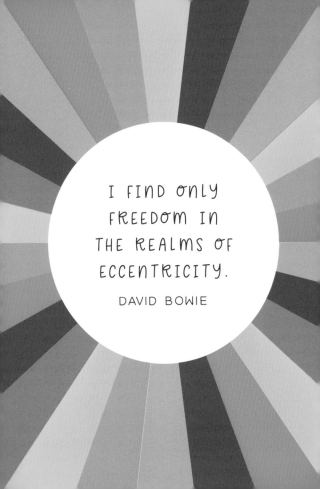

I FIND ONLY
FREEDOM IN
THE REALMS OF
ECCENTRICITY.

DAVID BOWIE

IF NOT
ME, WHO?
IF NOT
NOW, WHEN?

HILLEL THE ELDER

ACCEPT NOTHING
BUT THE FACT THAT
YOU'RE EQUAL.

NEKO CASE

SERVING WARRIOR PRINCESS REALNESS

IT'S OK TO
MAKE MISTAKES.
IT'S OK TO
FALL DOWN.
GET UP, LOOK
SICKENING, AND
MAKE THEM EAT IT.

LATRICE ROYALE

I AM MY OWN MUSE.

FRIDA KAHLO

WAKE UP, BEAUTY – IT'S TIME TO BEAST

There's nothing more badass than being who you are.

DARREN CRISS

LET YOUR INNER
QUEEN'S VOICE
COME THROUGH
LOUD AND CLEAR.
BE STRONG,
BE AUTHENTIC,
BE YOU, AND YOU'LL
DO HER PROUD.

QUEEN LATIFAH

WE CAME,
WE SAW,
WE BEDAZZLED!

CARSON KRESSLEY

YAAAS!

ALL OF US INVENT
OURSELVES. SOME
OF US JUST HAVE
MORE IMAGINATION
THAN OTHERS.

CHER

BE YOURSELF.
AN ORIGINAL IS
WORTH MORE
THAN A COPY.

SUZY KASSEM

DON'T
hide
YOUR
magic

THE IMPORTANT
THING IS NOT
WHAT THEY THINK
OF ME, BUT WHAT I
THINK OF THEM.

QUEEN VICTORIA

DO YOUR SQUATS, EAT YOUR VEGETABLES, WEAR RED LIPSTICK, DON'T LET BOYS BE MEAN TO YOU.

KENDALL JENNER

I'm strong.
I'm tough.
I still wear
my eyeliner.

LISA LESLIE

YOU
ARE
GOLDEN

I DON'T GET CUTE, I GET DROP-DEAD GORGEOUS.

ALYSSA EDWARDS

RIDE THE ENERGY
OF YOUR OWN
UNIQUE SPIRIT.

GABRIELLE ROTH

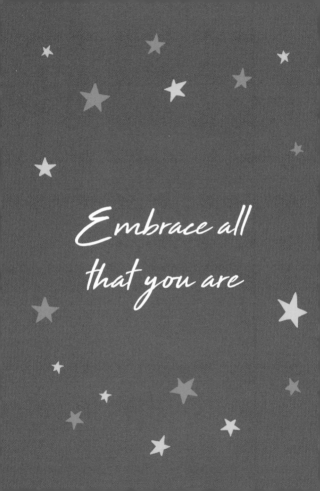

Embrace all
that you are

WHEN SOMEONE SAYS
YOU CAN'T DO IT,
DO IT TWICE AND
TAKE PICTURES.

ANONYMOUS

THE PRIVILEGE OF A LIFETIME IS BEING WHO YOU ARE.

JOSEPH CAMPBELL

I WON'T
CRY FOR YOU;
MY MASCARA'S
TOO EXPENSIVE.

ADRIANA LIMA

DAZZLE THEM, DARLING

NOT EVEN SHE COULD
HOLD HERSELF BACK
BECAUSE HER PASSION
BURNED BRIGHTER
THAN HER FEARS.

MARK ANTHONY

I'm not the next Usain Bolt or Michael Phelps. I'm the first Simone Biles.

SIMONE BILES

YOU'RE GIVING ME LIFE

IF YOU'RE ALWAYS TRYING TO BE NORMAL, YOU WILL NEVER KNOW HOW AMAZING YOU CAN BE.

MAYA ANGELOU

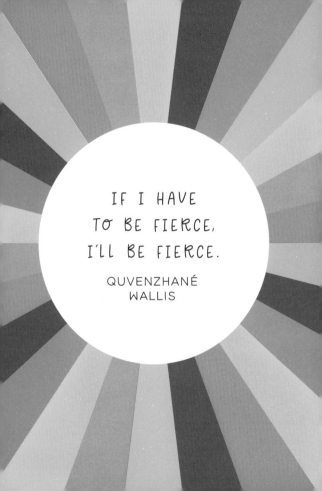

IF I HAVE
TO BE FIERCE,
I'LL BE FIERCE.

QUVENZHANÉ
WALLIS

I AM SOMEBODY.
I AM ME.
I LIKE BEING ME.
AND I NEED
NOBODY TO MAKE
ME SOMEBODY.

LOUIS L'AMOUR

MAKE IT HAPPEN!

BE FEARLESS,
BE BRAVE,
BE BOLD,
LOVE YOURSELF.

HARUKI MURAKAMI

A STRONG WOMAN
LOOKS A CHALLENGE
DEAD IN THE EYE AND
GIVES IT A WINK.

GINA CAREY

Sassy

since

birth

STILETTO, I LOOK AT
IT MORE AS AN ATTITUDE
AS OPPOSED TO A
HIGH-HEELED SHOE.

LITA FORD

You're perfect when you're comfortable being yourself.

ANSEL ELGORT

TRUE BELONGING
DOESN'T REQUIRE
US TO CHANGE
WHO WE ARE.
IT REQUIRES US TO
BE WHO WE ARE.

BRENÉ BROWN

OKURRR!

FOLLOW YOUR
INNER MOONLIGHT;
DON'T HIDE
THE MADNESS.

ALLEN GINSBERG

KNOW WHAT YOU'RE
WORTH AND DEMAND
THREE TIMES THAT.

TRIXIE MATTEL

LIFE TIP:
DO YOU

I'm not bossy.
I'm the boss.

BEYONCÉ

LIFE IS EITHER A
DARING ADVENTURE
OR NOTHING.

HELEN KELLER

**WHAT MATTERS
MOST IS HOW
WELL YOU WALK
THROUGH THE FIRE.**

CHARLES BUKOWSKI

SOME PEOPLE ARE JUST BORN WITH GLITTER IN THEIR VEINS

No one can make you feel inferior without your consent.

ELEANOR ROOSEVELT

I'D RATHER BE
LOUD AND
MISUNDERSTOOD
THAN QUIET
AND BORED.

ADAM LEVINE

Be you,
do you,
for you

WHEN YOU'RE
AROUND ME,
YOU'RE GOING TO
GET GLITTER
ON YOU.

KESHA

I DON'T GET BITTER.
I JUST GET BETTER.

RIHANNA

WHEN PEOPLE THROW SHADE, SHINE BRIGHTER!

FRANKIE GRANDE

BE A STILETTO IN A ROOM FULL OF FLATS

BE SO GOOD
THEY CAN'T
IGNORE YOU.

STEVE MARTIN

SOMETIMES YOU JUST HAVE TO PUT ON LIP GLOSS AND PRETEND TO BE PSYCHED.

MINDY KALING

ALWAYS WEAR YOUR INVISIBLE CROWN

*Make your
life the
masterpiece
you want
it to be.*

QUEEN LATIFAH

WHO YOU ARE AUTHENTICALLY IS ALL RIGHT... WHO YOU ARE IS BEAUTIFUL AND AMAZING.

LAVERNE COX

SHINE LIKE THE
WHOLE UNIVERSE
IS YOURS.

RUMI

FIERCEDOM, HONEY!

I CAN
AND I WILL.
WATCH ME.

CARRIE GREEN

BE STRONG,
BE FEARLESS,
BE BEAUTIFUL.

MISTY COPELAND

NEVER

lose

YOUR

sparkle

THE MOST IMPORTANT
THING IS TO LIVE
A FABULOUS LIFE.
AS LONG AS IT'S
FABULOUS I DON'T
CARE HOW LONG IT IS.

FREDDIE MERCURY

I WOULD RATHER BE A REBEL THAN A SLAVE.

EMMELINE PANKHURST

*It's all about
confidence and
how you feel
about yourself.*

HAYLEY HASSELHOFF

Make an entrance like you own the place

MY MISSION IN
LIFE IS NOT MERELY
TO SURVIVE, BUT TO
THRIVE; AND TO DO SO
WITH SOME PASSION,
SOME COMPASSION,
SOME HUMOR, AND
SOME STYLE.

MAYA ANGELOU

HAPPINESS AND CONFIDENCE ARE THE PRETTIEST THINGS YOU CAN WEAR.

TAYLOR SWIFT

YOU'RE A LIMITED EDITION

BE UNIQUELY YOU.
STAND OUT. SHINE.
BE COLOURFUL. THE
WORLD NEEDS YOUR
PRISMATIC SOUL!

AMY LEIGH MERCREE

LIVE, LOVE, LAUGH, LEAVE A LEGACY.

STEPHEN COVEY

I LOOK THOSE HATERS STRAIGHT IN THE EYE, KEEP MY CHIN UP AND SHOULDERS BACK. BECAUSE I KNOW I'M A FIERCE QUEEN – AND THEY KNOW IT, TOO.

ALYSSA EDWARDS

BEYONCÉ WASN'T BUILT IN A DAY

YOU DEFINE YOUR
OWN LIFE. DON'T LET
OTHER PEOPLE WRITE
YOUR SCRIPT.

OPRAH WINFREY

Some people
are so much
sunlight to the
square inch.

WALT WHITMAN

ANOTHER

day

ANOTHER

slay

IF YOU ASK ME WHAT
I CAME INTO THIS
LIFE TO DO, I WILL
TELL YOU: I CAME
TO LIVE OUT LOUD.

ÉMILE ZOLA

DARE TO
LOVE YOURSELF
AS IF YOU WERE A
RAINBOW WITH GOLD
AT BOTH ENDS.

ABERJHANI

ALWAYS BE
A LITTLE
UNEXPECTED.

OSCAR WILDE

YOU'RE
KILLING IT

IT'S NOT
YOUR JOB
TO LIKE ME.
IT'S MINE.

BYRON KATIE

A QUEEN KNOWS HOW TO BUILD HER EMPIRE WITH THE SAME STONES THAT WERE THROWN AT HER.

ANONYMOUS

I AM COMPLETELY COMPLETELY MYSELF – WHAT'S YOUR SUPERPOWER?

ALWAYS WEAR
AN INTERNAL CROWN
AND HAVE A
QUEENDOM MINDSET.

JANNA CACHOLA

Life is
about using
the whole box
of crayons.

RuPAUL

Pray,
slay,
conquer
the day

SOMETIMES YOU JUST HAVE TO THROW ON A CROWN AND REMIND THEM WHO THEY'RE DEALING WITH.

MARILYN MONROE

I DON'T KNOW
WHERE I'M GOING
FROM HERE, BUT
I PROMISE IT
WON'T BE BORING.

DAVID BOWIE

YAS
QUEEN

If you're interested in finding out more
about our books, find us on Facebook
at Summersdale Publishers and follow
us on Twitter at @Summersdale.

www.summersdale.com